GERMAN SHEPHERDS

Valerie Bodden

CREATIVE
PAPER BACKS

published by Creative Paperbacks
P.O. Box 227, Mankato, Minnesota 56002
Creative Paperbacks is an imprint of
The Creative Company
www.thecreativecompany.us

design and production by
Christine Vanderbeek
art direction by Rita Marshall
printed in the United States of America

photographs by Alamy (Vicki Beaver,
petographer, South West Images Scotland),
Corbis (Bettmann, JP Laffont), Dreamstime
(Paul Cotney, Isselee, Michha, Juan Carlos
Plaza Briones), iStockphoto (rusm, Martti
Salmela), Newscom (WALT DISNEY
PICTURES), Shutterstock (Eric Isselee,
Jagodka, Marcel Jancovic, Erik Lam,
Neveshkin Nikolay, Susan Schmitz, Viorel
Sima, Nikolai Tsvetkov, Kachiulkina Veronika,
WilleeCole)

library of congress
cataloging-in-publication data
Bodden, Valerie.
German shepherds / Valerie Bodden.
p. cm. — (Fetch!)
SUMMARY: A brief overview of the physical
characteristics, personality traits, and habits
of the German shepherd breed, as well as
descriptions of famous pop-culture shepherds
such as Rin Tin Tin.
Includes index.

ISBN 978-1-60818-362-3 (hardcover)
ISBN 978-0-89812-941-0 (pbk)
1. German shepherd dog—Juvenile literature.
I. Title.
SF429.G37B63 2014
636.737'6—dc23   2013005518

first edition
9 8 7 6 5 4 3 2 1

TABLE OF CONTENTS

Fetch!

SMART SHEPHERDS

A German shepherd is a *breed* of dog. German shepherds are smart, *loyal*, and brave. German shepherds love to work. They guard and obey their owners.

WHAT DO GERMAN SHEPHERDS LOOK LIKE?

German shepherds have long, muscular bodies. They have a long *muzzle* and dark eyes. Their pointy ears stand up. German shepherds' tails are long and bushy.

German shepherds have a good sense of hearing.

German shepherds are about two feet (61 cm) tall. They can weigh between 75 and 95 pounds (34–43 kg). A German shepherd's fur can be short, medium, or long. It can be straight or wavy. Most German shepherds are black and light brown. But some are all black or white and gray.

White German shepherds blend in with snow.

GERMAN SHEPHERD PUPPIES

Newborn German shepherd puppies weigh about one pound (0.5 kg). The puppies are born with floppy ears. The ears stand up straighter as the puppies get older.

Many German shepherds have all black or all tan fur at birth.

GERMAN SHEPHERDS IN MOVIES

German shepherds can be seen in movies and cartoons. In the Disney movie *Bolt*, Bolt the dog thinks he is a superhero. Bolt looks like an American white shepherd. American white shepherds look like white German shepherds. In some *Batman* comic books, Batman has a German shepherd named Ace the Bat-Hound.

Bolt's owner is a girl named Penny.

GERMAN SHEPHERDS AND PEOPLE

German shepherds are working dogs. More than 100 years ago, people began to use them to herd sheep. Today, German shepherds work as police dogs, military dogs, and guard dogs. Some guide people who are *blind*. Others are search-and-rescue dogs.

German shepherds help find people who are in trouble.

German shepherds are good with kids. German shepherd puppies make good pets for some people. But it can be a lot of work to train a puppy. Adult German shepherds do not need as much training. But they might have learned bad habits. Both male and female German shepherds make good pets. Females are usually smaller and quieter than males.

German shepherds are smart and learn quickly.

WHAT DO GERMAN SHEPHERDS LIKE TO DO?

German shepherds can live inside or outside.

They need a lot of exercise and time to explore.

German shepherds' fur should be brushed once

or twice a week.

Young German shepherds like to play and run.

German shepherds love to learn new things. Teach your German shepherd to sit, lie down, and shake hands. Then teach him to spin or to shake his head. You will both have fun!

A FAMOUS SHEPHERD

A dog named Rin Tin Tin was the most famous German shepherd ever. Rin Tin Tin starred in more than 25 movies in the 1920s. The dog was paid $1,000 a week and wore a diamond collar. He rode in his own *limousine*. People loved him so much that they sent him more than 10,000 fan letters a week!

GLOSSARY

blind unable to see

breed a kind of an animal with certain traits, such as long ears or a good nose

limousine a long, fancy car

loyal showing friendship for someone at all times

muzzle an animal's nose and mouth

READ MORE

Allen, Jean. *German Shepherds*. North Mankato, Minn.: Smart Apple Media, 2004.

Johnson, Jinny. *German Shepherd*. North Mankato, Minn.: Smart Apple Media, 2013.

Schuh, Mari C. *German Shepherds*. Minneapolis: Bellwether Media, 2009.

WEBSITES

Bailey's Responsible Dog Owner's Coloring Book
http://classic.akc.org/pdfs/public_education/coloring_book.pdf
Print out pictures to color, and learn more about caring for a pet dog.

Just Dog Breeds: German Shepherd
http://www.justdogbreeds.com/german-shepherd-dog.html
Learn more about German shepherds and check out lots of German shepherd pictures.

Every effort has been made to ensure that these sites are suitable for children, that they have educational value, and that they contain no inappropriate material. However, because of the nature of the Internet, it is impossible to guarantee that these sites will remain active indefinitely or that their contents will not be altered.

INDEX